Regional Guide

The Western Highlands and Islands of Scotland

Edmund Swinglehurst

Odhams Leisure Group
London · New York · Paris

Near Loch Ness on the Corrieyairack Road

A Land of Great Beauty

The Scottish Highlands are generally taken to include the high land north of a line between Dumbarton, near Glasgow, and Stonehaven on the east coast south of Aberdeen, but this book concentrates on the area west of the Great Glen and the Firth of Clyde.

This is a most wonderful region. In the spring limpid skies emphasise the vastness of the unspoiled countryside and the mountains stand out sharply against the horizon. The heather that covers the moors is burnt by the winter snow and seems like a rich brown fur over the landscape; in gardens and parks spring flowers grow profusely, encouraged by the warm air that comes in off the Gulf Stream. On the high mountains of Glen Coe and on Ben Nevis there are still vestiges of winter snow, and small lambs gambol over the open moors, protected, one hopes, from sudden accidents by signs along the roadside which read 'Lambs have no road sense'.

The main roads in Scotland are good at anytime, but in spring there is an added advantage in that there is little traffic, a fact which travellers particularly appreciate on those single-track roads which lead to many of the most beautiful and out-of-the-way places in the Highlands.

These single-track roads are quite a feature of the Highlands and are usually well maintained; passing places are marked with striped posts which enable you to gauge in advance where to pass or stop for an approaching car.

In summer, the Highland weather is less reliable than in spring or autumn, but this is still the main holiday season and the caravans and tents at the numerous west-coast sandy beaches suggest that there is enough sunshine to attract those who enjoy an open-air holiday. This is a time for swimming and sun-bathing, and also for walking, and if you do set off along some of the way-marked tracks you will meet plenty of others with the same idea.

Autumn is different again. The heather is now purple with bloom and the glens full of golden tints. The air is still warm and the skies clear. The days are shorter but long enough for a full day's touring and if the evenings are sometimes chill you may have the pleasure of a glass of malt whisky as you sit before a log fire.

To enjoy the best of the Highlands, a car and/or an energetic pair of legs (your own) are essential. You can, of course, take the train – and there are some beautiful rides – but the lines are limited to those from Inverness to Kyle of Lochalsh and Glasgow to Mallaig or Oban.

To get across to the Hebrides you can take a British Rail or Caledonian MacBrayne ferry or fly via British Caledonian or Loganair from Edinburgh and Glasgow.

To people who do not know Scotland, one of the pleasant surprises in store is the quality of the accommodation. Whether one stays in a simple bed-and-breakfast or in a former baronial hunting lodge like the Glen Garry Castle Hotel, the standards of cleanliness, friendly service and good and abundant food are always high.

Restaurants do not abound, but hotels welcome non-residents and at many of them the traveller can enjoy such Scottish traditional fare as Cock-a-leekie soup, Arbroath Smokies, trout, salmon, venison and Scottish bakery products such as oatcakes, scones and Dundee cake, often home-made.

In the summer months hotels and restaurants are usually crowded so it is always advisable to book rooms or reserve a table in advance.

Though the north-west Highlands of Scotland give the traveller a sense of freedom that is rarely found in the increasingly urbanised regions of Britain, distances between beauty spots or points of interest are relatively short. Within a range of 50 miles the traveller may find a castle, a loch, a mountain, forests, a crafts community or some other interesting features going back to the time of the Highland clans or even to the Iron Age. To enjoy travelling in Scotland to the full you should carry reasonably detailed maps of the area you are traversing; this will enable you to spot the beautiful and striking features of the landscape and make a car tour or walk all the more interesting, helping to establish firmly in the mind those images which make a holiday in the Scottish Highlands so memorable.

Highland cattle, with Liatach looming behind

The awesome ruins of Kilchurn Castle on Loch Awe; the keep was built by Sir Colin Campbell of Breadalbane in 1440

Strathclyde and the Trossachs

At first glance, the fragmented region of south-west Scotland known as Strathclyde seems too spaced out to include in one visit. The land is strung out in long peninsulas or islands separated by lochs across which there are few ferries. The northern part of Strathclyde has good roads which make it accessible to motorists and there are ferries to the islands of Bute and Arran. The long peninsula of Kintyre west of Arran does require a special expedition; you must go down its length and return up it – though by a different road if you wish. Jura and Islay also are islands that are difficult to fit into a tour. They must be regarded as places for a special visit.

The difficulty of communication or of fitting several destinations on one tour should not discourage you from visiting this rich and beautiful part of western Scotland. There is enormous variety here from the popular beauty of Loch Lomond and the Trossachs to the wild mountainous shores of Arran. Any journey will be full of unexpected surprises.

There are also attractive and interesting towns and villages like Rothesay, Dunoon, Inveraray and Campbeltown, and carefully tended gardens such as at Achamore on Gigha Island off Kintyre, Arduaine House on Loch Melfort and at Crarae Lodge on Loch Fyne. It is a legendary land, too, with the memory of Rob Roy's exploits still able to stir the imagination on Loch Lomond and the story of the last of the Picts, who preferred death by jumping off a cliff at the Mull of Kintyre to revealing the secret of heather ale, reminding one that Scotland was inhabited before the Scots arrived.

Route 1: The Trossachs

Glasgow, Aberfoyle, Stronachlachar, Inversnaid, Trossachs Hotel, Brig O'Turk, Callander, Lake of Menteith, Glasgow. Distance: approx. 90 miles.

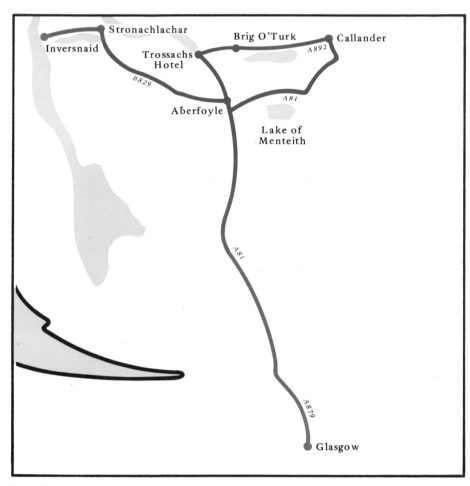

A mere 30 miles separates the industrial city of Glasgow from the miniature highlands of the Trossachs, a region of lochs and forests of exceptional beauty.

From *Glasgow*, take the A81 to *Aberfoyle*, passing Campsie Fells which rise to 1800 feet on the right of the road north of Strathblane.

At Aberfoyle, a busy gateway town for the Trossachs, this route turns west on to the B829 through the Pass of Aberfoyle to Inversnaid on Loch Lomond. On the way, you pass 3192-foot Ben Lomond and Lochs Ard and Chor in an open expanse of moorland. Also on the route, about 11 miles from Aberfoyle, is *Stronachlachar* on the western end of Loch Katrine. There is a well-kept waterworks here surrounded by giant firs and pines. This is good walking country: a path round Loch Katrine to the Trossachs Hotel at the eastern end (about 10 miles) makes a good walk.

At *Inversnaid*, reached by a minor road west from Stronachlachar, there is a good view across Loch Lomond and you can visit Rob Roy's cave where the MacGregors used to meet before their raids on the surrounding country.

From Inversnaid, return to Aberfoyle and take the A821 to the *Trossachs Hotel* on Loch Katrine, from where you can board a steamer, the *Sir Walter Scott*, for a loch tour to Stronachlachar.

From the Trossachs Hotel, the route on the A821 continues to *Brig O'Turk* on Loch Venachar and then on to *Callander*. The drive is through countryside celebrated in Sir Walter Scott's novels *Rob Roy* and *The Lady of the Lake*.

Callander is regarded as a gateway to the Highlands. To the north the landscape becomes more rugged; to the south the A81 goes through farmlands on its return to Glasgow via Aberfoyle.

About 7 miles south of Callander, the A81 skirts the north shore of the *Lake of Menteith*. On the island in the lake is Inchmahome Priory where Mary, Queen of Scots, took refuge after the Scots' defeat at the Battle of Pinkie and before her escape to France where she married the dauphin of France.

The remains of the 13th-century church contain various Stewart tombs and the tomb of R. B. Cunninghame Graham, the colourful writer who spent much of his time in Argentina.

The Maid of the Loch *passes Ben Lomond on Loch Lomond*

The Trossachs Hotel, a splendid Victorian baronial pile at the western end of Loch Archray

Steamer trips on Loch Katrine are a big attraction for visitors to the Trossachs

Route 2: Campbell Country

Inveraray, Clachan, Cairndow, Arrochar, Tarbet, Ardlui, Crianlarich, Tyndrum, Bridge of Orchy, Dalmally, Cladich, Inveraray. Distance: approx. 70 miles.

The Campbells, earls and dukes of Argyll, were good survivors during the turbulent period when warfare was destroying the clans like the MacDonalds and the McLeods who fought each other and the English, to their cost. The result was that Campbell country extended over much of south-west Scotland and included Loch Awe and Loch Fyne. The headquarters of the Campbells is *Inveraray*, a most attractive village built on the shore of Loch Fyne in the 18th century when the 3rd Duke of Argyll decided to separate the village from his castle, and the starting place for this drive through Campbell country.

The work of John Adam, the 18th-century architect, can be seen at the Argyll Arms and at the Town House. Inveraray Castle, which is just outside the town, was badly damaged by fire in 1975 but was rebuilt and can be visited. Its interior is sumptuous, and includes tapestries, fine china, 18th-century paintings and a good collection of old masters.

From Inveraray, the route takes the A83 north-east up Loch Fyne to *Clachan* and then down to *Cairndow*, a run of about 11 miles. The A83 now climbs up Glen Kinglas into typically Scottish mountain scenery, passing Beinn an Lochain (2992 ft) on your right and Ben Ime (3318 ft) on the left, with Ben Donich (2774 ft) straight ahead. At the top of the pass is a stone engraved with the words 'Rest and Be Thankful', a thought which before the days of motor cars must have expressed the feelings of many footsore travellers.

The road now follows another glen, Croe, down to Loch Long past the Cobbler, otherwise 2891-foot Ben Arthur, and so-called because its shape suggests a shoemaker bending over his last, through the village of *Arrochar* then over a short pass to *Tarbet* on Loch Lomond. Thus, in the 12 miles or so from Cairndow to Tarbet our route has encompassed two glens, three lochs and miles of superb Scottish mountain scenery.

The A82 now skirts the western shore of the loch in the lee of Ben Vorlich (3092 ft) north to *Ardlui* at the head of the loch to enter a wild and bare mountain area along Glen Falloch and so down into *Crianlarich*, a junction of the Oban-Fort William railway. From here, the route follows the A82 to *Tyndrum*, from where you can either drive down Glen Lochy on the A85 or carry on north on the A82 towards *Bridge of Orchy*, turning left on to the B8074 to drive down the beautiful

Inveraray Castle, seat of the dukes of Argyll, head of the Clan Campbell

Glen Orchy whose river flows over stone outcrops in a series of falls and rapids.

The Glen Orchy road joins the A85 near *Dalmally*, and our route continues on the A85 to *Loch Awe*, at whose head stands the impressive ruins of Kilchurn Castle, once the home of Colin Campbell of Breadalbane. During this 15th-century warrior's frequent absences at wars, his virtuous wife extended and strengthened the castle. A very splendid spot this, with Beinn Mhic Mhonaidh (2602 ft) and Beinn Eunaich (3242 ft) dividing the landscape to the north.

From the castle, take the A819 down the south side of Loch Awe and fork left at *Cladich* and, keeping to the A819, return to Inveraray via Glen Aray.

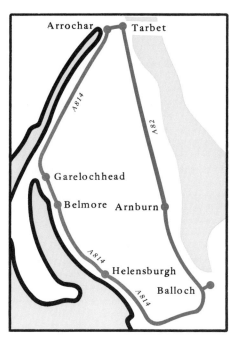

The harbour at Tarbert, Argyll

Pleasure craft at Balloch on Loch Lomond

Route 3: Loch Lomond Country

Balloch, Arnburn, Tarbet, Arrochar, Garelochhead, Belmore, Helensburgh (or Glen Fruin), Balloch. Distance: approx. 45 miles.

Balloch, at the southern end of Loch Lomond, is a popular place where a private park, complete with deer, bears, bison and other animals, was once the home of the Smollets whose most famous son was Tobias Smollet, the author. From Balloch pier the *Maid of the Loch* offers frequent cruises on Loch Lomond.

Our route from Balloch takes the lakeside road to the A82, which runs up the west shore of Loch Lomond. From the road there are lovely views of the broad southern end of the loch with its many wooded islands: then the loch narrows, with Ross Point reaching across from the far shore. Further north, 3192-foot Ben Lomond on the east shore and Ben Vorlich on the west provide some dramatic scenery.

This is MacGregor and Colquhoun country, where they had their last strongholds against the Hanoverian kings. At *Arnburn*, 5 miles north of Balloch, is Rossdhu, the home of the Colquhouns. It was rebuilt in the 18th century and the work is thought to have been carried out by Robert Adam.

There are lovely views all the way up the loch as far as *Tarbet*, where you can turn left for *Arrochar* on Loch Long and follow the road down the east side of the loch to *Gareloehhead* and then *Helensburgh*. If you wish you can fork left at Belmore, just south of Garelochhead, bypassing Helensburgh and going down Glen Fruin, scene of a great battle between the MacGregors and Colquhouns over cattle rights. Cross the B832 for the way back to Balloch via the B831 and the A82. (From Helensburgh, take the B832 back across to the A82 and so back south to Balloch.)

7

Gazetteer

ABERFOYLE
Busy village, centre for walkers and motorists exploring the Trossachs and the Hills of Menteith. Pony trekking from the Inn; several nature trails.

Visit:
Ben Lomond (3192 ft). A 10-mile walk from Aberfoyle, but it can be shortened by taking a car to Loch Ard and starting the walk there;
Inchmahome Priory, 4 miles E of Aberfoyle, on island in Lake of Menteith, reached by ferry in summer. Open daily (exc Thur, Fri, Oct-Mar) all year;
Stronachlachar at the western end of Loch Katrine.

ARRAN
Mountainous island that embodies every feature of Scottish Highland landscape, reached by car ferry from Ardrossan to Brodick, all year and from Claonaig on Kintyre to Lochranza, summer only.

Visit:
Blackwater Foot and the King's Caves on the west side of the island where Robert Bruce rested and where he saw the spider;
Brodick Castle (NTS) open daily Apr-Sept, garden and country park open all year;
Glen Rosa, beauty spot north of Brodick;
Lochranza Castle, where Robert Bruce is said to have landed from Ireland to begin his campaign for Scottish independence. Open daily all year.

ARROCHAR
Small village at the head of Loch Long with plenty of accommodation for visitors.

BALLOCH
Village at southern end of Loch Lomond. Loch cruises from pier on *Countess Fiona*.

Visit:
Cameron House for Smollet library museum, and Cameron Wildlife Park, both at Cameron Loch Lomond, open daily Apr-Oct.

BALQUIDDER
At the eastern end of Loch Voil. Home of Rob Roy MacGregor.

Visit:
The Old Kirk and the graves of Rob Roy, his wife and sons.

BUTE
Island south of the Cowal peninsula, and west of Glasgow. Car and passenger ferry from Colintraive to Rhubodach at the northern end, and from Skelmorlie to Rothesay, the island's capital.

Visit:
13th-century Rothesay Castle, now ruin but once the centre of Stewart operations against the Lords of the Isles;
St Mary's Chapel, ruined chapel with tombs of two Stewart kings.

CALLANDER
Lovely old town surrounded by wooded hills beyond which lie Highland moors.

Visit:
Ben Ledi (2875 ft) on W side of Callander – a three-hour (4 miles) climb from Coilantogle on the A821;
Falls of Bracklinn, 1 mile from Keltie Water, reached by footpath from Callander;
The Pass of Leny and its gorge 2½ miles NW on the way to Lochearnhead.

The elegant drawing room at Cameron House, the family home of the Smollets, near Balloch

CAMPBELTOWN

Founded by James IV and passed on to the Argylls in 1618. This town is a long way down the Kintyre peninsula but can be reached by steamer from Glasgow. There is also an air connection.

Visit:

Davarr Island, connected to the mainland by a sandbank;
St Keiran's cave, 3 miles S of Campbeltown.

CRINAN

Yachting centre on the Sound of Jura and the western exit of the Crinan Canal which was built by John Rendle between 1743-1801.

Visit:

Cairnbaan, SE, to see ruined Dunadd Fort, once the capital of ancient Dalriada. Open at all reasonable times.

DUNOON

A popular resort on the Cowal peninsula facing east into the Firth of Clyde. Two good bays for bathing and sailing.

Visit:

The Castle. Little remains of the old castle of the Argylls but there is a good view. The 19th-century castle houses a collection of old photographs;
Holyloch, 2 miles NW of Dunoon. At the head of the loch is Younger Botanic Garden, an annex of the Edinburgh Royal Botanic Gardens, open daily Apr-Oct.

INVERARAY

Campbell headquarters on Loch Fyne. An attractive 18th-century town of white and pink buildings surrounded by wooded hills. The old Town House on the front is by John Adam and the Argyll Arms, once known as the Great Inn, was the pub where Dr Johnson and Boswell stayed and first sampled Scotch whisky.

Visit:

Inveraray Castle, gothic-style building erected between 1744-1785 and added to in Victorian times as well as being restored after a fire in 1975. The original architect was Roger Morris who employed William Adam, father of Robert and John. Tapestries, paintings and furniture and much interesting plaster work. Open daily July-Aug, and daily exc. Fri, Apr-June, Sept-mid-Oct;
Crarae Gardens at Crarae Lodge 4 miles down the west side of the loch. Open daily Mar-Oct.

ISLAY

Low-lying island west of Kintyre with good beaches for an away-from-it-all holiday. Big famous-name malt whisky

Brodick Castle, ancient seat of the dukes of Hamilton, on Arran

industry.

Visit:

Bowmore Round Church, built by the Campbells of Shawfield in mid-18th century, its shape perhaps owed to the belief that without corners, evil spirits would have nowhere to hide. Open daily to dusk;
Kildalton Crosses in Kildalton churchyard, 7 miles NE of Port Ellen, are two very fine Celtic crosses;
Museum of Islay Life, at Port Charlotte, open daily Apr-Sept, Mon-Fri, Oct-Mar.

JURA

Mountains, the Paps of Jura, rise in the south of this island. Loch Tarbert, half way across the island, almost cuts it in two. Boat excursions from Ardlussa to the whirlpools and tidal race of Corrievreckan.

LOCHGILPHEAD

Small Victorian village of white houses built along single main street and round the head of Loch Gilp. Crinan Canal runs parallel to loch past the village.

TARBERT

Tiny fishing village between Knapdale and Kintyre on Loch Fyne. Departure point for steamers to Jura, Colonsay and Islay, and the Hebrides.

Visit:

Gigha Island off the Kintyre peninsula, reached by steamer from Tarbert, has lovely gardens at Achamore House, open daily all year.

Around Oban and Mull

The land between Loch Awe and Loch Leven and including the island of Mull is the old Kingdom of Lorn of which Oban was the capital. It is a place full of dramatic clan history, of legends and of fine scenery including mountains like Ben Cruachan and narrow defiles like the Pass of Brander and rugged Glen Coe.

The Macleans, MacDougalls and MacDonalds as well as the Campbells all struggled for control of the castles here, and Glencoe was not the only massacre to take place amid the dark hills.

To travel in this region is like taking a journey through a romantic novel, with every page revealing an exciting and thought-provoking visit to times past.

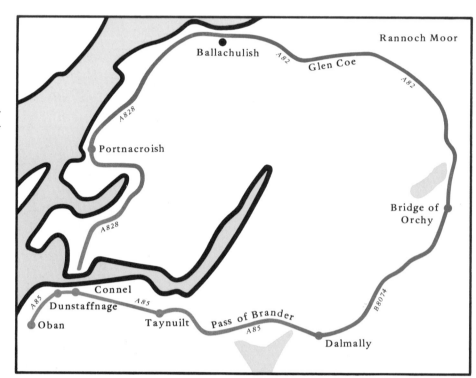

Route 1: The Glen Coe Circuit

Oban, Dunstaffnage, Connel, Taynuilt, Pass of Brander, Dalmally, Bridge of Orchy, Rannoch Moor, Glen Coe, Ballachulish, Portnacroish, Connel, Oban.
Distance: approx. 107 miles.

From *Oban* this route takes the A85 which climbs over the protecting hills to the north and descends towards Dunbeg and impressive *Dunstaffnage Castle*, captured by Robert Bruce, struggled over by Stewarts and MacDougalls and once the prison of Flora Macdonald. The castle, 4 miles north of Oban, looks out over Ardmucknish Bay into which Loch Etive flows over the Falls of Lora at *Connel*. The A85 continues for 8 miles along the south side of the loch to *Taynuilt*, an ancient iron foundry town where guns for Nelson's ships were made. There are good views from here up Loch Etive, the north-east arm of which can only be visited on foot or by boat.

The A85 now climbs through the exciting *Pass of Brander* whose rocky sides slide down to the clear waters of Loch Awe. On the pass road is the entrance to the impressive hydro-electric station buried deep inside Ben Cruachan in a vast cave dug out for it.

As the lake opens up, you may see Kilchurn Castle rising in lonely splendour on the loch side. The A85 passes the farm gates leading to the castle on the way to *Dalmally*. Here, the route turns left on to the minor road B8074 up lovely Glen Orchy with its boulder-strewn river shaded by trees and heather-covered hills.

At *Bridge of Orchy* the route joins the A82 which crosses the wild expanse of *Rannoch Moor* to Glen Coe. Superb ranges of mountains dominate the horizon all around, including Buachaille Etive Mor (3345 ft), the Great Herdsman of Etive.

Loch Leven, with the bare peak of the 2430-foot Pap of Glencoe rising behind

Penetrating *Glen Coe* is always a thrilling experience – rain or shine. The road descends through vast brooding mountains to the spot where the massacre of the MacDonalds took place in 1692, and then enters a green valley leading to Loch Leven. There is an excellent National Trust for Scotland Visitor Centre at the bottom of the pass.

Glencoe village is charming and popular. From here the A82 follows the southern shore of Loch Leven to *Ballachulish* where it joins the A828 which runs along Loch Linnhe, circling inland past *Portnacroish*, where Castle Stalker stands proudly on its rock off-shore, and round Loch Creran to join the A85 at Connel for Oban.

Many skiers know Blackrock Cottage on Rannoch Moor, since it sits by the path to a popular Glen Coe chair-lift

The Kinghouse Hotel on the River Etive is a familiar landmark on the way to Glen Coe. Sron na Creise is the hill behind the hotel

11

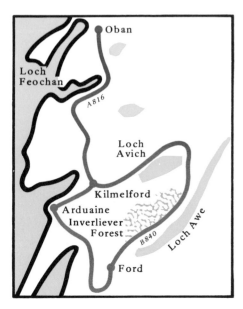

Route 2: Around Loch Awe
Oban, Loch Feochan, Kilmelford, Loch Avich, Inverliever Forest, Ford, Arduaine, Loch Feochan, Oban. Distance: approx. 54 miles.

This route entails some slow travel along minor roads once you leave the A816. From *Oban*, the A816 goes inland south over pretty wooded country for 15 miles to *Kilmelford* near which Carnasserie Castle stands on a commanding position above the road.

At Kilmelford, the route turns left at the hotel off the A816 and along a minor road to *Loch Avich*. If travelling in spring-time, make sure the road is passable before you start.

After passing Loch Avich, you enter the Forestry Commission's Inverinan Forest of conifers. Across the loch, the Eredine Forest, a naturally wooded area with deciduous trees, spreads across the skyline.

Turning right on to the Loch Awe road, you pass through the *Inverliever Forest* which climbs up into the gentle hills surrounding the southern extremity of *Loch Awe*. *Ford* is a small village where the roads that descend each side of the loch join up.

Through Ford, the route continues along the B840 to the A816, turning right for *Arduaine* where Arduaine House, on a promontory by Loch Melfort, formerly a Campbell residence and now a hotel, has fine gardens open to the public and expansive views of the loch.

Passing *Loch Feochan* on your return to Oban, watch out for the many wild swans that frequent this sheltered spot.

McCaig's Tower sits like some strange crown over the harbour at Oban

The pretty harbour front at Tobermory, the largest resort on Mull

Route 3: The Island of Mull

Craignure, Salen, Tobermory, Calgary,
Uskamull, Killichronan, Loch Scridain,
Fionnphort, Iona, Glen More, Duart,
Craignure. Distance: approx. 130 miles.

The car ferry ride from Oban to Mull is
full of interest. The Caledonian
MacBrayne ferry slides out of Oban Bay
past the northern point of Kerrera Island
with Dunollie Castle standing out on the
starboard bow. Halfway across the Firth
of Lorne is Lismore Island and a small
rock called the Lady's Rock where
Maclean, Lord of Duart, whose castle
can be seen on a rocky mount of Mull,
left his wife to die.

The ferry docks at *Craignure*, where
our route takes the A849 north to *Salen*,
an attractive little village with Aros
Castle on the north side of the bay. At
Salen a road goes across the narrowest
3-mile-wide part of Mull to its western
shore.

The A848 carries on up the Sound of
Mull for 10 miles to picturesque
Tobermory, surrounded by wooded hills

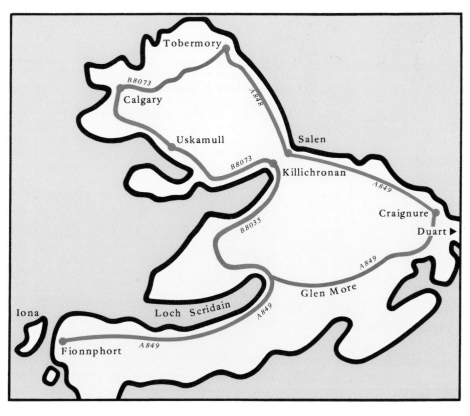

and with a harbour usually crowded with boats. Legend, perhaps supported by fact, has it that a Spanish Armada galleon laden with gold lies at the bottom of the bay.

From Tobermory, the B8073 goes westward to *Calgary*, emigrants from which founded Calgary in Canada. The road now turns south with wonderful views of Ulva and the other islands off western Mull. As you skirt the north shore of Loch Na Keal which penetrates deeply into Mull towards Salen, you will have good views of Ben More (3169 ft) on the southern shore.

If you want only a short drive round Mull you can now drive back to Salen, and then to Craignure, 16 miles away. If not, take the B8035 between *Killichronan* and *Gruline* and continue along the south side of Loch Na Keal around Ben More to *Loch Scridain*. Here the A849 goes to *Fionnphort*, embarkation point for the island of *Iona*. The island, with its abbey and tombs of Scottish kings, has a magic that attracts visitors from all over the world. Return on the A849 through some pretty countryside, including *Glen More*, to Duart Point where Duart Castle, including its dungeons, can be visited.

Sheep graze peacefully on the slopes above the cathedral on Iona, where St Columba landed in 563

Grim Duart Castle, seat of the Macleans of Duart, has dominated the Sound of Mull for seven centuries

Gazetteer

ARDUAINE
Lovely gardens on a peninsula of Loch Melfort, 20 miles SW of Oban near pleasant hotel with views of the loch from its restaurant. Gardens open Sat-Wed, Apr-Oct.

BALLACHULISH
Village by main exit of Loch Leven into Loch Linnhe. Look out for the monument to James Stewart of the Glens, hanged at Ballachulish on suspicion of murdering Colin Campbell, the 'Red Fox', who was evicting Stewarts from this part of the country.

BEN CRUACHAN
Dominates rocky Pass of Brander. The vast underground power station here is open daily, Easter-Oct.

BENDERLOCH
Small village on south shore of Loch Creran.

Visit:
15th-century Barcaldine Castle where an 18th-century Stewart of Appin fought and killed Duncan Campbell of Glen Orchy. Stewart, fearing the revenge of the Campbells, chose to go straight to their castle at Loch Awe and ask for hospitality, knowing that once given the host could not harm his guest. That night the ghost of the murdered Campbell reproached his brother for not killing his foe and foretold his death at Ticonderoga in America. The prophecy was fulfilled and the Loch Awe Campbell returned to haunt his castle to this day. Castle open by arrangement Easter, July-Oct (tel. Ledaig 214);
Barcaldine Forest, along the A828, has well-marked paths for some attractive walks. Car parking just south of Benderloch Post Office.

CASTLE STALKER
Ancient house of Stewarts of Appin, stands on a tiny rock in Loch Laich off Portnacroish and facing Loch Linnhe. Open by appointment Mar-Sept (tel. Upper Warlingham 2768).

CRAIGNURE
Mull's ferry terminal. 10¼in gauge steam railway operates from Old Pier.

Visit:
Torosay Castle, splendid Scottish baronial-style house in terraced gardens. Open Mon-Fri, mid-May-Oct and Sun, July-Aug.

DUART CASTLE
Great keep stands on a rock at the eastern edge of Mull, built by the Lords of the Isles in 13th century and now the home of the Macleans. Open daily, May-Sept.

DUNSTAFFNAGE CASTLE
The stone of destiny once lay in this square castle which guards the entrance to Loch Etive, 4 miles N of Oban. The castle is on a peninsula and is open daily except Friday all year. In the 14th century, Sir John Stewart, near death with only an illegitimate son as his heir, decided to marry his mistress and thus legitimise his son. At the wedding, Campbells and Macdougals tried to kill him, but Stewart lived long enough to complete the ceremony.

The car ferry from Fionnphort to Iona

GLEN COE
Brooding glen between wild Rannoch Moor (2000 ft) and the mouth of Loch Leven, guarded at its western end by 3345-ft Buachaille Etive Mor, and with impressive mountains along it. From The Study is a fine view of the glen.

Visit:
Clen Coe Visitor Centre (NTS), open daily Apr-mid-Oct;
Glen Coe and North Lorn Folk Museum, open Mon-Sat, May-Sept.

IONA
Island one mile off Fionnphort at the SW corner of Mull. Accessible by frequent ferry services from Fionnphort or direct from Oban.

Visit:
Site of monastery founded by St Columba AD563 and burial place of Scottish kings; island now home of the Iona Community;
Staffa Island with strange basalt columns (Fingal's Cave), by boat from Iona or steamer from Oban.

LISMORE
10-mile-long island in Loch Linnhe about ¾ mile from the mainland. A central road runs down the spine of the island and there are the ruins of 3 castles. A monastery was founded here by St Molnag in the 6th century.

LOCH AWE
Long inland loch which once reached the sea via what is now the Pass of Brander. At upper part of the loch Kilchurn Castle can be viewed from the outside only.

LOCH ETIVE
Beautiful loch, legendary home of Deirdre of the Sorrows. (She had to leave it to join her betrothed, King Conchobar in Ireland. Her friends, the sons of Uisneach, followed but were killed by King Conchobar: Deidre died of a broken heart.) At the mouth of Loch Etive are the Falls of Lora caused by an underwater outcrop of rock seen only at low tide.

OBAN
Popular west-coast town, capital of Lorn, whose most distinctive feature is McCaig's Tower, a mock-Roman folly dominating the town. George Street, with shops, restaurants and hotels, runs parallel to the harbour. The ruins of Dunollie Castle, closed to the public, are on the outskirts of town. The 2-mile-long esplanade, overlooking the bay, is lined with hotels and guest houses. Excursions by steamer to Mull, Isle of Staffa, Hebrides, Coll, Tiree and Colonsay and Lismore.

Visit:
The Dog Stone, near Dunollie Castle, is large stone pillar where Bran, the hound of Fingal, was supposedly tied;
McDonald's Mill, where spinning and weaving exhibited. Open daily all year;
Oban Glassworks, open Mon-Fri all year, plus Sat, May-Sept;
Pulpit Hill for view of harbour.

TAYNUILT
Attractive village on Loch Etive. Boats from pier take visitors to beautiful Upper Loch Etive.

Visit:
Hamlet of Bonawe, once Britain's main iron-smelting centre. Cannon were cast here for Nelson's ships. Bonawe Iron Furnace open daily Apr-Sept.

TOBERMORY
Mull's largest resort, where picturesque harbour lined with 18th-century houses, quayside piled with lobster pots and enough shops to keep the thousands of summer visitors happy, make this attractive village memorable. Boats for hire for cruise into Sound of Mull; ferries to Oban, Coll, Tiree and the Hebrides.

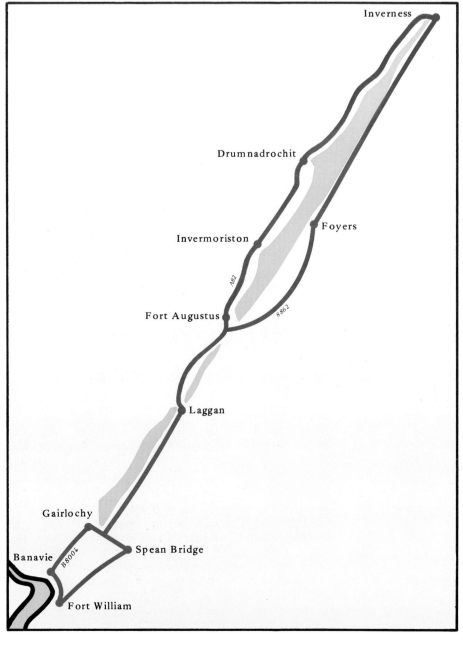

The Great Glen

The Great Glen cuts across Scotland from Loch Linnhe in the south-west to the Moray Firth in the north-east, linking Loch Ness, Loch Oich, Loch Lochy and Loch Eil. Most of the rivers that flow into it come from the north, where many lochs and valleys lead into the Highlands. To the south, the Great Glen is flanked by a ridge of hills with one major break at Glen Roy.

The Caledonian Canal, which follows the line of the Glen, was built by Thomas Telford between 1803 and 1822. The canal made it possible for waterborne traffic to cross from the North Sea to the Irish Sea and vice versa. Today it is used largely by pleasure boats. Its 29 locks include Neptune's Staircase, a series of 8 locks at Banavie at its southern end.

Route 1: The Great Glen
Fort William, Banavie, Gairlochy, Laggan, Fort Augustus, Invermoriston, Drumnadrochit, Inverness, Foyers, Spean Bridge, Fort William.
Distance: approx. 135 miles.

From *Fort William* this route takes the A82 north, turning left on to the A830 towards Glenfinnan, and then right to Banavie after crossing the River Lochy. The road, the B8004, climbs through trees past Neptune's Staircase on the Caledonian Canal at *Banavie.*

From here the road goes to *Gairlochy,* where there are good views of Ben Nevis from the canal lock. At Gairlochy, the road crosses the river to Spean Bridge, with lovely scenery overlooking the Spean River. At the junction with the A82 stands a fine monument to the Commandos. Our route follows the A82 along the south-eastern edge of Loch Lochy, and there are many good views across the loch to the wooded north bank. At *Laggan,* the road crosses to the north side of Loch Oich, a small pretty loch near whose southern end stands the Well of the Seven Heads. An obelisk decorated with seven men's heads and built over a spring, the Well marks the spot where the heads of the seven murderers of the sons of Keppoch, head of the MacDonells, were washed before being presented to the grieving father. An account of this vengeance appears on the obelisk in Gaelic, English, French and Latin.

A mile further up Loch Oich is one of the prettiest spots in the Great Glen. The River Garry enters the loch at this point and runs parallel to the loch along a wooded peninsula on which is the Glengarry Castle Hotel. In the hotel's grounds is ruined Invergarry Castle, one of the places where Bonnie Prince Charlie stayed before Culloden.

After Loch Oich, which also has its monster, the A82 comes to *Fort Augustus*

This lock on the Caledonian Canal at Fort Augustus gives access to Loch Ness

and Loch Ness. The Fort, built by General Wade during the 18th century, was later presented to the Benedictine Order who founded a handsome abbey there.

Six miles up Loch Ness is *Invermoriston* where the northern branch of the Road to the Isles goes up Glen Moriston. Another 11 miles brings our route to Urquhart Castle, an extensive picturesque ruin on the loch's edge. This is as good a spot as any to look for the Loch Ness Monster, since it is supposed to have its lair under the castle. From nearby *Drumnadrochit*, the Glen Urquhart road leads up the glen to Glen Urquhart Forest and lovely Glen Affric.

The A82 continues north along Loch Ness to *Inverness*, a fine town and capital of the Highlands. The return to Fort William can be made along the south shore of Loch Ness along the B862 and the B852, which turns inland at the Falls of Foyers to rejoin the B862 for Fort Augustus.

Beautiful Glen Affric, watered by the River Affric flowing through two lochs

Sad reminder of Britain's last land battle

Leanach Farmhouse on Culloden Moor, the Jacobite headquarters before the battle

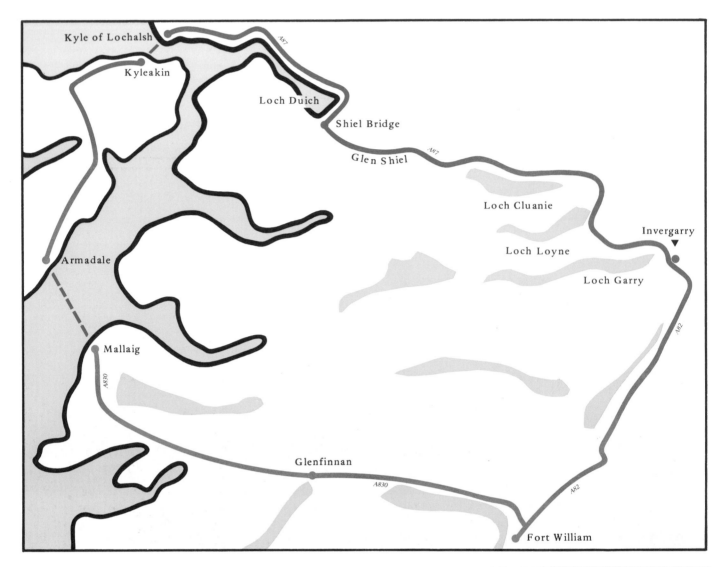

Route 2: The Roads to the Isles

Fort William, Invergarry, Loch Garry, Loch Loyne, Loch Cluanie, Glen Shiel, Shiel Bridge, Loch Duich, Kyle of Lochalsh, Kyleakin, Armadale, Mallaig, Glenfinnan, Fort William. Distance: approx. 139 miles.

There are two roads to the Isles from the Great Glen; this route includes one of them on the outward trip and one returning, from Mallaig.

From *Fort William*, the route takes the A82 25 miles north to *Invergarry* on Loch Oich and turns left on to the A87 up wooded Glen Garry. There are extensive walks through the Glen Garry Forest. The road now climbs above *Loch Garry*, offering splendid views, and comes out into the bare hills around Loch Loyne. Keeping to the A87, and skirting the north shore of *Loch Cluanie*, the route descends Glen Shiel, an impressive gorge of huge boulders and towering cliffs, to Loch Duich. The mountains on the right are known as the Five Sisters.

At *Shiel Bridge* at the head of Loch Duich, a minor detour to Ratagan Forest is well worth doing if you have the time. Another detour could take you up the minor road at Morvich from where there is a good walk up the valley to the Falls of Glomach.

Our main route, still on the A87, now goes along Loch Duich to Eilean Donan Castle, crosses Loch Long at Dornie and continues along the wooded shores of Loch Alsh to *Kyle of Lochalsh*, where the short ferry crossing to *Kyleakin* on Skye begins.

(A more scenic route is by the old road which goes higher up the hill of Keppoch, via a turning up from Loch Duich past Inverinate, from which there are superb views of the upper loch. The road then descends towards Dornie, giving you a bird's eye view of Eilean Donan Castle, before carrying on to Kyle of Lochalsh.)

Once on Skye, the route from Kyleakin takes the A850 to Broadford, turning off on to the A851 to reach *Armadale,* from where in summer the Armadale-Mallaig ferry crosses the Sound of Sleat back to the mainland.

From *Mallaig*, the route takes the A830 down the coast to inland Loch Morar and on south past Loch nan Uamh and Loch Ailort. The A830 now heads inland to *Glenfinnan* at the head of Loch Shiel, the place where Bonnie Prince Charlie rallied the clans in 1745. A statue of a kilted Highlander on the column by the loch's edge recalls the event. There is an excellent National Trust for Scotland Visitor Centre here with good facilities

Invergarry Castle on Loch Oich

and a mural telling the Bonnie Prince Charlie story. A little way up the valley, Thomas Telford's splendid railway viaduct is a fine landmark.

From Glenfinnan, it is a short pleasant run to Fort William along the northern shore of Loch Eil and around the head of Loch Linnhe.

Eilean Donan Castle stands near Dornie on the edge of Loch Duich, facing down Loch Alsh

These mountains edging Loch Duich are known as the Five Sisters

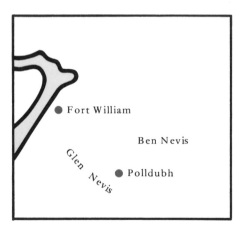

Route 3: The Ben Nevis Walk
Fort William, Glen Nevis, Polldubh,
Ben Nevis.

To reach Glen Nevis, you take the A82 north out of *Fort William*, turning right on to the minor road for Glen Nevis at *Nevis Bridge*. The glen is a wide green valley with woods on the right and the western slopes of Ben Nevis to the left. A track to the left takes you to *Achintee farm*, starting point for the usual route to the top of Ben Nevis, a four-hour walk along a stony track which passes a mountain loch and then zigzags to the summit.

This route misses some of the beauty of the glen and we suggest that you continue up the glen by car to *Polldubh*, near which is a car park.

From here, continue on foot up the most spectacular part of the glen through a gorge with 400-ft sides on which pines and birches and other trees cling precariously. On the right some way up the gorge is a fine waterfall. The track arrives at Loch Treig, nearly 12 miles from Polldubh, after crossing the watershed of the Water of Nevis and Abhainn Rath.

There is no way up Ben Nevis on this route for non-experienced climbers; therefore if you wish to reach the summit return to Achintee farm.

The climb up Ben Nevis, though practicable for any normally fit person, is hard work and requires stout shoes and clothing appropriate for bad weather as the sunshine in which you start can soon turn to cloud, rain and strong winds. Particular care should be taken in spring when there is still snow on the route.

The view from the summit is superb, taking in the Cairngorms to the east, the Glen Coe mountains to the south, Ben Cruachan by Loch Awe, the Cuillin hills of Skye and the Hebrides.

Gazetteer

BEN NEVIS
At 4406 feet, this is Britain's highest mountain. It is one of a group of mountains which includes Carn Dearg (3348 ft) and Carn Mor Dearg (4012 ft). From the west Ben Nevis looks like a large rounded hump but from the east the cliffs and gullies give it a more dramatic appearance. The best view is from Spean Bridge.

CULLODEN
The battlefield 5 miles E of Inverness on which Bonnie Prince Charlie's Highlanders were defeated on 16 April 1746 by the Duke of Cumberland, later christened 'Butcher' Cumberland because of his ruthless treatment of the Highland people. Parts of the moor are now planted with trees and others are farmed but there is enough of it left to enable one to picture the battle, which lasted less than an hour, and in which 1200 Highlanders were slain.

Visit:
National Trust for Scotland Visitor
  Centre, open daily mid-Apr–mid-Oct.

The British Isles' highest mountain, 4406-feet Ben Nevis, dominates the countryside near Fort William

DRUMNADROCHIT
Village on 24-mile-long, 700-feet-deep Loch Ness.

Visit:
Loch Ness Monster Exhibition Centre which tells the story of Britain's most famous monster. Open daily in peak tourist season, various times rest of year (to check, tel. Drumnadrochit 573);
Urquhart Castle, 2 miles SE on Loch Ness. 'Nessie' is supposed to have her lair beneath the castle's extensive ruins. Open daily all year.

FORT AUGUSTUS

Busy village at the southern end of Loch Ness. Has many hotels and is frequented by tourists, walkers and fishermen. There are good walks from the village, especially along the old military roads, one of which goes up the Corrieyairack Pass to Laggan.

Visit:
Fort Augustus Abbey which incorporates General Wade's Fort. Guided tours daily by arrangement (tel. Fort Augustus 6232);
The Great Glen exhibition which includes Loch Ness monster section. Open daily Apr-Oct.

FORT WILLIAM
One of the busiest resorts in the Highlands as it gives access to Ben Nevis, the Great Glen and the Roads to the Isles. The original fort after which it was named, built by Cromwell's General Monk, no longer exists but there are the remains of a castle at Inverlochy and a hotel of the same name though of later date.
The main street of Fort William is also the A82 main road so the town is always busy with traffic.

Visit:
Ben Nevis Centre, High Street, open daily all year;
Caledonian Canal, whose southern end is at Corpach, near Fort William. The famous flight of 8 locks, Neptune's Staircase, is at Banavie, 3 miles NW of Fort William;
The Museum, housed in an 18th-century house, contains among other Highland exhibits the 'secret' portrait of Bonnie Prince Charlie.

GLEN FINNAN
A glen leading to Loch Shiel. The spot where Bonnie Prince Charlie rallied the clans in 1745 is marked by a column on which the statue of a Highlander stands and which can be climbed by an internal spiral staircase.

Visit:
National Trust for Scotland Visitor Centre, Glenfinnan, open daily Apr-mid-Oct.

GLEN GARRY
On the A87 between Loch Oich and the Kyle of Lochalsh. The A87 climbs out of the loch through trees towards Loch Loyne; a minor road continues along Loch Garry. The scenery is extremely beautiful and gets wilder as the valley leads on to Loch Hourn, a little-visited but most beautiful loch on the west coast.

GLEN SHIEL
Comparable to Glen Coe in its beauty, Glen Shiel connects Loch Cluanie and Loch Duich. Bonnie Prince Charlie spent a night in the Glen under a rock now known as Clach o' Phrionsa, the Prince's rock.

INVERNESS
The busy capital of the Highlands at the mouth of the River Ness is a centre for visitors to the Grampians and the northern Highlands. The Picts had a town here. The town's first castle, long destroyed, was where Macbeth killed Duncan. The second castle, on Castle Hill, was blown up by Bonnie Prince Charlie.

Visit:
Abertarff House, Church Street, 16th-century building housing Highland culture exhibition. Open Mon-Sat all year;
Craig Phadraig, vitrified fort 1½ miles W on hill overlooking Beauly Firth;
Exhibition of the Scottish Highlander, Hentley Street, open daily Apr-Sept;
Inverness Museum and Art Gallery, Castle Wynd, open Mon-Sat all year;
Muirtown locks for cruises on Loch Ness.

KYLE OF LOCHALSH
Loch Alsh separates the mainland from the Isle of Skye. The Kyle is the embarkation point for the car and passenger ferry. A busy place in summer, Kyle of Lochalsh has a good hotel and several shops and cafes.

Visit:
The Balmacara Estate, 8000 acres of parkland belonging to the National Trust for Scotland. The idyllic village of Plockton on Loch Carron is on the estate.

SPEAN BRIDGE
An important junction of the A82 and A86 with a bridge built by Telford.

Visit:
The commando monument, the work of Scott Sutherland. Fine views of Ben Nevis from here.

Inverness Castle, the most recent of several castles on the site: Bonnie Prince Charlie blew up the previous one in 1745

Skye and the Hebrides

Although only half a mile from the mainland at its eastern extremity, the Isle of Skye has an individual and isolated character that gives it a special atmosphere. The island is 60 miles long, deeply indented by sea lochs and most of its interior is rugged although there are sheltered valleys where trees and green fields provide a satisfying contrast.

On the south side of the island are the famous Cuillin Hills, much painted by Victorian artists and today a favourite territory for walkers and climbers. To the north are the peninsulas of Trotternish, Vaternish and Duirnish stretching out into the Little Minch which lies between Skye and the Outer Hebrides.

The island was the scene of struggles between the MacLeods, the MacDonalds and the MacKinnons and later of these clans against the Hanoverians. Flora Macdonald, who helped Bonnie Prince Charlie to escape his pursuers, lived and is buried on the island, which today attracts thousands of visitors from all over the world during the summer months.

The Outer Hebrides, or 'The Long Island' as this 130-mile-long collection of small islands off the west coast of Scotland is known to the local Scots, can be reached by ferry from Uig in northern Skye, as well as from Ullapool and Oban on the mainland. Well worth exploring, with their superb sandy beaches, rugged coastlines and bare dramatic hillscapes, the Outer Hebrides remain a colourful outpost of the old Gaelic Scotland.

Route 1: Southern Skye
Kyleakin, Broadford, Sligachan, Drynoch, Glen Brittle, the Cuillin Hills, Kyleakin. Distance: approx. 80 miles.

The ferry from Kyle of Lochalsh takes only a few minutes to cross the half-mile stretch between Skye and the mainland. The scenery is lovely here, with ruined Castle Moil over-looking the strait from the Skye side and, on the mainland, the wooded hills of Lochalsh stretching inland to Loch Duich.

From *Kyleakin* the route takes the A850 to *Broadford*, passing Skye airport, 8 miles away. (Just before the small village of Broadford, there is a left turn on to the A851, to Armadale, the ferry point for Mallaig on the mainland while from Broadford itself you can do a 14-mile detour to Elgol, a village surrounded by cliffs overlooking Loch Scavaig and with views of the offshore islands of Canna, Rhum and Eigg. It was at Elgol that the MacKinnons sheltered Bonnie Prince Charlie during his post-Culloden odyssey.)

From Broadford, our route continues along the A850. The road winds between the mountains and the sea to the *Sligachan Hotel*, a popular stopping place for mountaineers and walkers, to whom the hotel supplies useful information, including leaflets on local walks, as well as all the usual hotel amenities.

The A850 goes on to Portree, but our route turns off along the A863 over rough moorland surrounded by mountains to *Drynoch* on Loch Harport on the south-west side of Skye.

From here, the narrow B8009 goes towards Carbost, our route turning off a mile or so before the village along a single track road to *Glen Brittle* which skirts the Cuillin Hills and eventually arrives at Glenbrittle House on Loch Brittle, a popular starting point for climbs into the Cuillins.

The return to Kyleakin is along the same route. The route to Portree is via the A850 from Sligachan.

Route 2: Northern Skye
Portree, The Storr, Flodigarry, Kilmuir, Uig, Blackhill, Dunvegan, Bracadale, Sligachan, Portree. Distance: approx. 80 miles.

Since *Portree*, Skye's capital, is the place that most tourists make for on an overnight stop on the island, it is sometimes difficult to find accommodation here. Even so, the town is strangely untouched by its visitors. The Portree people remain attached to their traditional ways of life, even to the point of refusing to take in bed-and-breakfast customers on the eve of the Sabbath. The character of the people of Skye adds to the attraction of the town and a visit here is always memorable.

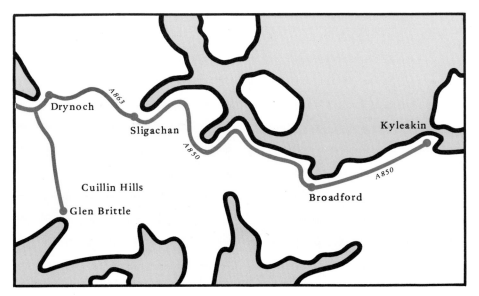

Armadale Castle on Skye, built early in the 19th century, houses the Clan Donald Centre

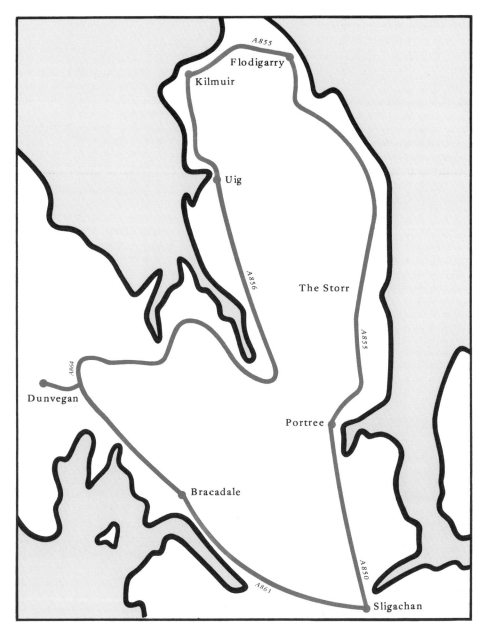

Dunvegan Castle, on Skye

dominated by the seat of the MacLeods, Dunvegan Castle, which still stands rather forbiddingly on its rocky outcrop which was once an island. Today, a bridge joins the castle and its pretty gardens. The present castle dates from the 15th century with additions in subsequent centuries until the 19th. The great keep and the dungeons are 16th-century.

In the great hall, now the drawing room, are the tattered remnants of the Faery Flag which the MacLeods received from a fairy spirit who promised them success in battle and male heirs as long as they owned the flag.

Across Loch Dunvegan lies the Duirnish peninsula which can be explored along a single narrow road which goes along the western side of Loch

The centre of activity is the cobbled square and the Royal Hotel where Bonnie Prince Charlie said goodbye to Flora Macdonald.

From Portree, the route takes the A855 north along the coast. About 8 miles north of Portree, and near the northern end of Loch Leathan, is the *Old Man of Storr*, a black column, 160 feet high, on the side of The Storr. Further on, at Quirang, there are more stony pillars and the road then goes on to *Flodigarry*, where Flora Macdonald and her husband lived.

From here, the A855 curves with the coastline and turns south along Loch Snizort, past the ruins of Duntulm Castle, which can be seen from the road, and the monument to Flora Macdonald, who is buried at *Kilmuir*, less than a mile further on. At *Uig* is the port of embarkation for the Outer Hebrides.

The A856 runs along Snizort Beag, the upper part of Loch Snizort, before meeting the A850 which takes our route west along the base of the Vatternish peninsula via *Blackhill* to *Dunvegan*,

Among the rocks of The Storr, Skye: the Cuillins lie beyond

Dunvegan to Idrigill Point. Here, three stone stacks standing out to sea represent the wife and two daughters of a MacLeod chief who were drowned at sea. On the way, at *Colbost*, is a Black House Museum which represents the life of crofters and displays the utensils and implements of their daily life.

Driving south from Dunvegan, on the A863, you can either head for Sligachan along the west coast, with fine views of the lochs and islands and thus be well placed for returning to Kyleakin, or you can turn off the A863 at *Bracadale* on to the B885 for Portree.

Route 3: The Outer Hebrides
Stornoway, Tarbert, Stornoway.
Distance: approx. 72 miles.

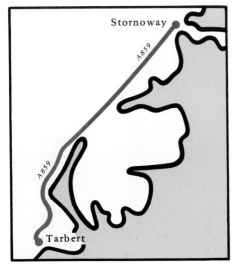

The Outer Hebrides consist of several islands including Lewis, Harris, North Uist, Benbecula, South Uist and Barra. It is difficult to see the islands in less than one week but short trips can be made from the mainland to explore at least some of them and to get a taste of these lonely outposts of Britain.

Caledonian MacBrayne ferries leave from Ullapool for Stornoway on Lewis and from Uig for Tarbert on Harris, or you could take a British Airways flight from Glasgow or Inverness. There is also a Caledonian MacBrayne route from Uig to Lochmaddy on North Uist. The company's service to South Uist and Barra is from Oban.

One suggested route to discover something of these lovely islands is from Stornoway. The A859 takes you south through a flat landscape full of lochans to North Harris, where hills and mountains stretch to the sea in the west and on to Loch Tarbert which, but for a narrow isthmus, would make South Harris into an island.

Tarbert is a small, pretty port surrounded by hills. Beyond it to the south, the A859 continues along the west coast of Harris to Rodel at the south-east tip, where there is a fine panorama of cliffs and rocks and with views across to the northern peninsulas of Skye.

North Uist, Benbecula, Grimsay and South Uist are all linked by one main road, with ferry crossings between them. It was Bonnie Prince Charlie's stormy crossing of the Little Minch from Benbecula to Skye which inspired the famous 'Skye Boat Song'.

Stornoway, chief town on Lewis, the northernmost of the islands of the Outer Hebrides

Castlebay on Barra, dominated by ancient Kisimul Castle

Gazetteer

BARRA
The most southerly of the larger Outer Hebridean islands. Can be reached by car ferry from Oban. The island is 8 miles long and 4 miles wide, and its main harbour is Castlebay in the south.

Visit:
Kisimul Castle, on island in Castlebay, dates from 12th century. Open Wed, Sat, May-Sept.

BENBECULA
Outer Hebridean island between North and South Uist with a flat and indented shore. The A865 from North to South Uist crosses the island, which has a small airport. Bonnie Prince Charlie and Flora Macdonald went over the sea to Skye from the south of the island.

CANNA, EIGG, RHUM AND MUCK
Four islands to the south of Skye. There is a round trip to the islands from Mallaig by Caledonian MacBrayne. Canna is the northernmost island of the group and is only 4½ miles by ¾ mile in size. Eigg and Rhum are larger, Rhum

having a large nature reserve where the habits of red deer have been studied over several years. Muck, like Eigg, is privately owned and its land is used for grazing and farming.

DUNTULM
Small village in the north of Skye, at the north-east corner of the Trotternish peninsula, notable for ruins of Duntulm Castle, home of the MacDonalds, Lords of the Isles. The ruins are said to be haunted by the ghost of a daughter of the house, bewailing her murdered lover.

DUNVEGAN
Pleasant village in the north of Skye.

Visit:
The Castle, the seat of the MacLeod chiefs for over 700 years and now a favourite tourist stopping place. Much of the interior was refurbished in the 19th century. Letters of Sir Walter Scott and Dr Johnson are on display. The trap door to the dungeons where a party of Campbells was murdered in one grizzly episode in the castle's history is kept open during visiting hours. Open daily, exc. Sun, Apr-Oct.

KYLEAKIN
Ferry terminal on the Isle of Skye for Kyle of Lochalsh. Kyle Akin was named after a 13th-century King Hakon of Norway who passed that way with his soldiers during an attempt to conquer Scotland. The Norsemen were defeated at Largs.

MALLAIG
Small port at the end of the road and rail service from Port William; ferry to Armadale in Skye.

Visit:
Loch Scavaig and the Cuillin Hills by
  steamer from Mallaig;
Loch Hourn by motor boat;
Knoydart by motor boat: walkers like
  this solitary peninsula.

PORTREE
Named Portree, 'Port of the King', after a visit by James V. Pretty fishing port and biggest town on Skye. Boat excursions leave from the harbour.

RAASAY
Thin, 15-mile-long island to the north-east of Skye. The ruins of Brochel Castle, former home of the MacLeans where Bonnie Prince Charlie hid during his wanderings after Culloden, can be seen.

STORNOWAY
Chief port of Lewis, centre of the fishing industry. Alexander MacKenzie, discoverer of the Mackenzie river in Canada, was born here.

Wester Ross

North from Loch Alsh the western Highlands become wilder and more austere; ranges of rocky mountains run from south-east to north-west and strips of lochs cross the Highlands to the Firth of Cromarty.

In contrast to the bare grandeur of the mountains, there are also green valleys, gardens and sandy bays which, despite attracting thousands of visitors during the summer months, remain peaceful in the away-from-it-all solitude.

Along the coast are rocky peninsulas reaching out into the Little Minch; inland, there are lochs accessible only on foot and plentiful wildlife: deer and wildcats, eagles and martens and rivers full of trout and salmon.

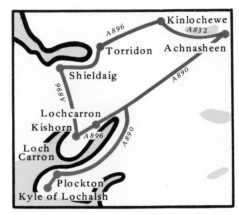

Route 1: Around Torridon
Kyle of Lochalsh, Plockton, Lochcarron, Kishorn, Shieldaig, Torridon, Kinlochewe, Achnasheen, Loch Carron, Kyle of Lochalsh. Distance: approx. 102 miles.

From *Kyle of Lochalsh* this route takes the minor road north crossing National Trust for Scotland land over the hills for 5 miles to *Plockton*, an idyllic village popular with artists. The minor road continues east along Loch Carron to just south of *Stromeferry* where it joins the A890. There is a pleasant run to the head of the loch where the A890 joins the A896, which this route follows by turning left to Lochcarron village and then 4 miles over the hills to *Kishorn* at the head of Loch Kishorn. Some 10 miles further north, still on the A896, you come down into Upper Loch Torridon, with a breath-taking view before you as you approach *Shieldaig*, turning right here to carry on along the south shore of the loch to Torridon village.

There is a good walk from the village along the north side of the loch past Torridon House and over the pass to Diabaig which overlooks Loch Diabaig, an arm of outer Loch Torridon.

The motoring route continues up Glen Torridon along the A896, with 3456-foot Liathach on the left and Sgurr Dubh (2566 feet) to the right. Then, as the valley opens towards Kinlochewe, the majestic form of Beinn Eighe appears on the left.

At *Kinlochewe*, a village at the junction of the A896 and A832, the route turns right for *Achnasheen* 9 miles away, passing Loch a' Chroisg from which rises the River Bran, named after Fingal's legendary hunting hound who, so it is said, dug out the valley with his paws.

At Achnasheen the route turns right along the A890 for the way south to Glen

An idyllic corner of Plockton on Loch Carron

Glen Torridon borders the spectacular mountain region of the Beinn Eighe Nature Reserve and the Torridon Estate

Loch Coulin, with the Beinn Eighe range to the north

Carron. There is a railway along the Glen in which the River Carron pours its tumultuous way via three lochs to the lower valley where it meanders down to the sea loch. The return to Kyle of Lochalsh is made by the southern shore of *Loch Carron*, Stromeferry and Lochalsh.

From Lochcarron, on the northern shore of the loch, it is possible to make a scenically splendid detour to the Applecross peninsula which lies to the west between Loch Kishorn and Loch Torridon. A minor road off the A896 climbs spectacularly over the Bealach-na-Bà up 1:4 gradients and there are good views of the pass eastwards. As you descend on the western side you should see the islands of Scalpay and Raasay off the north-east coast of Skye and the Cuillin hills showing up clearly. The road now descends to the Applecross Forest and to the village of Applecross, one of the remotest inhabited regions of Wester Ross. From Applecross a minor road goes north around the bay and the coast of the peninsula to Shieldaig.

Route 2: Around Gairloch

Gairloch, Poolewe, Aultbea, Gruinard Bay, Little Loch Broom, Dundonnell, Falls of Measach, Glascarnoch, Strath Bran, Loch a'Chroisg, Kinlochewe, Loch Maree, Gairloch. Distance: approx. 97 miles.

From the pretty and popular resort of *Gairloch* with its splendid beach, the route takes the A832 6 miles to *Poolewe*, a crofting village in a green valley at the head of Loch Ewe. Less than a mile along the edge of the loch are Inverewe Gardens, created by Osgood Mackenzie in 1862 and one of the wonders of Wester Ross. Much of the earth had to be imported to create the gardens which, due to the sheltered situation, are rich in plants usually found in more southern latitudes.

From Inverewe the A832 climbs above the loch and then descends to *Aultbea*, a scattering of houses overlooking the Isle of Ewe and a popular yachting rendezvous.

The A832 now climbs through a rocky cleft to a viewpoint above *Gruinard Bay* which is fringed with sandy beaches. It is well worth while stopping here to admire the view of the bay and the island. Gruinard Island cannot be visited, for it was used for World War II experiments with anthrax and still carries a risk of contamination.

Beyond Gruinard House, the road crosses to *Little Loch Broom* and runs along the south side of the loch with fine views of Beinn Ghobhlach (2082 ft) to *Dundonnell*, a small village with a good hotel, the starting point for walks to An Teallach (3483 ft).

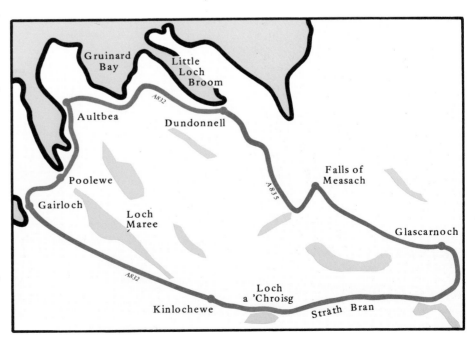

The A832 joins the A835 from Loch Broom near the Corrieshalloch Gorge, 13 miles from Dundonnell. There is a narrow footbridge which allows a good view of the *Falls of Measach* as they plunge 150 feet down the gorge. The route now continues eastward along the A835 between the 3536-feet-high mountain Beinn Dearg to the north and Sgurr Mor (3637 ft) to the south. The road climbs through pretty scenery to *Loch Glascarnoch*, an artificial lake created in 1950 as a hydro-electric reservoir. It improves the scenery of Diridh Mor, the Great Ascent, as the pass is called. The road descends to Garve, but our route turns right just before arriving at the village on to the A832 to *Strath Bran*, down which runs the railway fron Inverness to Kyle of Lochalsh.

The road climbs over the pass to *Achnasheen* and *Loch a'Chroisg* and *Loch Maree*, one of the handsomest lochs in Scotland. The loch has many wooded islands, one of which was sacred to the Druids and later was lived in by St Maelrubha. On the northern shore, 3217-foot Slioch dominates the scenery.

There is a right-of-way along the south shore, providing a walk along the wooded edges of this beautiful loch. Towards the western end of the loch, the road climbs away through coniferous forests and then drops down to Kerrysdale and Gairloch.

Gazetteer

GAIRLOCH
A large village with sandy beaches and a golf course. Several hotels cater for holiday visitors.

Visit:
Gairloch Heritage Museum, open Mon-Sat, Easter-Sept;
Port Henderson, small fishing village on the south shore of outer Loch Torridon (take the B8056 from Kerrysdale south of Gairloch);
Rubhe Reidh peninsula which stretches out between Gair Loch and Gruinard Bay.

GARVE
Small village on the railway from Inverness to Kyle of Lochalsh. Starting point for walks up Ben Wyvis (2497 ft).

GRUINARD BAY
A pretty bay ringed with beaches, popular with campers in summer. The island is out of bounds owing to anthrax contamination.

KINLOCHEWE
Small village which is good base for visits to Loch Maree and Beinn Eighe.

Sand-fringed Gruinard Bay lies north of Gairloch

Visit:
Beinn Eighe Nature Walk. A mile along A832 lies Loch Maree with Slioch (3217 ft) to the north accessible only to walkers. Beinn Eighe nature walk is here. Deer, eagles, wildcats, and many varieties of birds. Drive along A896 for about 6 miles and walk up stalker path between Liathach and Beinn Eighe.

LITTLE LOCH BROOM
The younger sister of Loch Broom is not lacking in its own grandeur.
An Teallach (3483 ft) rises behind Dundonnell House and Hotel and across the loch is Beinn Ghobbied (2082 ft).

LOCHCARRON
Well kept, former fishing village with white houses and flowering gardens strung along the north side of Loch Carron. From the pass on the way to Kishorn on the A896 there are superb views of the loch, the Applecross road and the Cuillin Hills of Skye.

LOCH MAREE
11 miles long, wooded loch with several islands. Isle Maree is the site of the hermitage founded by St Maelrubha. Its spring was reputed to cure insanity. Two crosses on the island, legend says, mark the graves of a Norwegian prince and princess. He feigned death to test her love and she killed herself in grief. Discovering the dreadful result of his ruse, the prince also killed himself.

MEASACH, FALLS OF
In the spectacularly narrow Corrieshalloch Gorge through which the River Droma tumbles on its way to Loch Broom. There are paths along the edge of the gorge, a viewing platform, a suspension bridge for walkers and good car-parking facilities.

PLOCKTON
One of the prettiest villages in Wester Ross. Popular with artists, its white houses look out over the loch.

POOLEWE
Village at the head of Loch Ewe. Popular centre with several small hotels.
Visit:
Inverewe Gardens: National Trust for Scotland wooded gardens with plants from all the world's temperate regions. See the famous 35-foot Magnolia Campbelli. Gardens open all year;
Fionloch – far-away-from-it-all walk to the loch; there are no roads, but there is a track (6 miles) from the Pool House Hotel.

TORRIDON
Small village in the magnificent surrounds of Loch Torridon under National Trust for Scotland care. Plenty of wildlife.

Visit:
Deer Museum, open daily, June-Sept.

The North-West Highlands

In spring and autumn the light that fills the huge expanses of sky in the north-west Highlands transforms the landscape. The wide open spaces of moorland seem to stretch for miles and the mountains appear higher than their actual 3000 feet or so.

In the great emptiness of the north, there is a strange magic and a feeling of adventure. Here among the rugged sea lochs along the coast where seals and seabirds gather, you feel as if you are on the edge of the universe.

Though there are few roads and many of these are single-track with passing places, the going is good but not fast – but who wants to hurry in such breathtaking surroundings?

Ullapool on Loch Broom, now a resort town, was founded as a herring fishing centre in 1788

Route 1: The Coigach Mountains
Ullapool, Drumrunie, Inverkirkaig, Lochinver, Loch Assynt, Inchnadamph, Ledmore, Ullapool.
Distance: approx. 61 miles.

Ullapool on Loch Broom is a good centre for a north-west Highlands holiday. The old herring port has several good hotels and it provides easy access to the wonders of the north-west.

Our first route in this region takes the A835 north out of Ullapool towards Ardmair on the shore of Loch Kanaird. Here you get a foretaste of the Coigach mountains with Ben More Coigach (2438 ft) rising steeply into the sky across the loch.

The route goes through Strathkanaird to *Drumrunie*, turning left on to a minor road to Inverkirkaig. The scenery is exciting: on the right is Cul Beag (2523 ft) and then the cone of the 2009-foot Stac Pollaidh (or 'Polly') with its shattered crown. Between the two is the walk to the Inverpolly Nature Reserve and Loch Sionascaig. The road itself stays by Loch Lurgainn's edge to its western end where there is a fork, the road to Achiltibuie which overlooks the Summer Isles turning to the left, and the Inverpolly Lodge road to the right. Both roads are single track but passing places are frequent and well marked. Our road takes the right turning, entering Sutherland at *Inverkirkaig*. Just off the road, which takes a sharp bend as it crosses the river, is an isolated house where you can buy guide books, knitted wear, sheepskins and other Scottish presents. A walk up the River Kirkcaig brings one to Fionn Loch.

Lochinver, a village in a superb setting of sea and mountains in the north-west highlands

The road now wends its way inland for a couple of miles to *Lochinver*, a scattered village of white houses round a protected natural harbour on Loch Inver used by fishing boats and overlooked by a large hotel. There is a good view of the 2399-foot Suilven's great dome shape rising inland from across the harbour. The walk to the mountain begins at Lochinver.

From Lochinver, the A837 follows the River Inver east to *Loch Assynt* over a wild rocky, mountain-gashed terrain. At the eastern end of the loch, 11 miles from Lochinver, stands ruined Ardvreck Castle where the Scottish leader Montrose sought refuge in 1650. He was betrayed and sent for trial and execution at Edinburgh.

The A837 joins the A894, which the route originally left at Drumrunie, just north of the castle and turns south to *Inchnadamph*, a good angling centre, behind which rises the wall of 3273-foot Ben More Assynt. To the west lies Canisp (2779 ft).

There are good views all the way back to Ullapool including those of Cul More (2786 ft) and Stac Polly.

Route 2: The Heart of the North-West

Lairg, Altnaharra, Loch Loyal, Tongue, Loch Eriboll, Durness, Rhichonich, Laxford Bridge, Scourie, Kylstrome, Loch Assynt, Ledmore, Oykel Forest, Loch Shin, Lairg. Distance: approx. 135 miles.

Loch Shin runs from north-west to south-east in the centre of the north-west Highlands. At its southern end a dam faces *Lairg,* an attractive village with a good hotel set by the River Shin which flows eastward through the Shin Forest. Lairg is something of a Highland junction, since roads from north, south, east and west all pass through it.

This route leaves the A836 in a northerly direction, coming after 2 miles or so to a right fork to Altnaharra. The road climbs over desolate moorland to the lonely village of *Altnaharra* by Loch Naver which empties down Strath Naver, one of the valleys cleared of crofters when the ill-advised Duke of Sutherland of the early 19th century drove the inhabitants out of their homes in order to give the land over to sheep raising. Many Scots were driven abroad to find new homes in North America, Australia and New Zealand in the course of these infamous 'Highland Clearances'.

Altnaharra must be one of the loneliest places in the north-west, but it has a certain grandeur in its wild setting in the lee of Ben Klibreck (2367 ft). The A836 continues north past *Loch Loyal* with fine views of Ben Loyal (2504 ft) and Ben Hope (3040 ft) to the pretty village of *Tongue* where there are two good hotels.

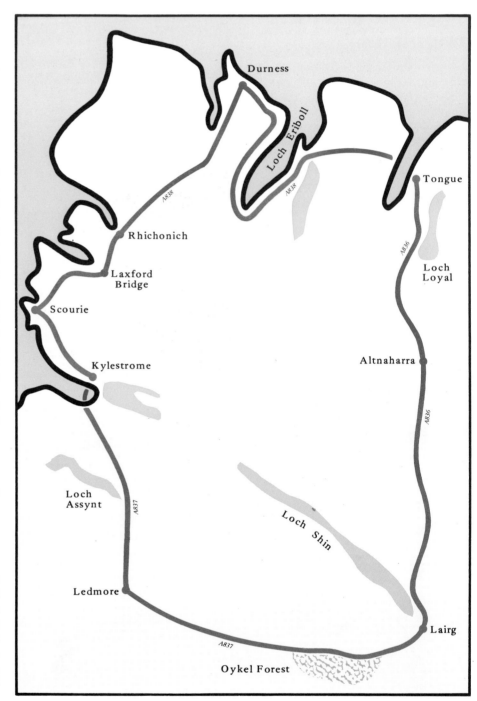

Loch Shin, 16½ miles long, is a hydro-electric reservoir

The Falls of Shin, on the River Shin south of Lairg, and a popular place for watching salmon leap

Empty beaches for miles near Durness in the far north of Sutherland

The view from Tongue across the Kyle of Tongue to the old Mackay Castle Varrich is very fine. The Kyle can be crossed by a causeway but it is more interesting to take the older road round the head of the Kyle and so on to the A838.

The route now crosses to *Loch Eriboll*, with Ben Hope on the left showing its craggy, precipitous northern face. The route circles Loch Eriboll, a very beautiful sea loch with cliffs and rocks on which seals bask. There are plenty of signs of early habitation here, brochs, hut circles and even a complete earth house by the roadside north of Laid.

West of the mouth of Loch Eriboll near *Durness* is the Smoo Cave, a three-chambered cave into the second of which falls an 80-ft high waterfall: an impressive sight worth a visit.

From Durness, the A838 turns south along the Kyle of Durness. A short side road takes you to Keoldale where there is a passenger ferry across the Kyle of Durness to connect with a minibus service to Cape Wrath.

Continuing south-west along the A838 over wild and solitary moorland, the route comes to *Rhiconich*, 15 miles from Durness at the head of Loch Inchard, where there are a few houses and one hotel. (From Rhiconich a road leads out along the north side of the loch to Kinlochbervie, an important fishing port set among crofts on the slopes of the lochside hills. There is a further track from here leading to Sheigra, a crofting community looking out over The Minch.)

From Rhiconich, the A838 goes on 4 miles to *Laxford Bridge*, another small community at the head of the very indented Loch Laxford, full of islands. Beyond Rhiconich, a minor road to the left leads to Tarbet, the nearest point to Handa Island, a bird sanctuary in the care of the British Society for the Protection of Birds, on which guillemots, kittiwakes, razorbills, fulmars, puffins and other sea birds can be seen in large numbers. The island can be visited by boat from Tarbet.

Further south along the A894 and 26 miles from Durness is the small community of *Scourie*, set in a small attractive green valley and with a pleasant hotel, very welcome to tired travellers.

Sixteen miles further on through the Reay Forest, once the hunting ground of the Mackays but now almost treeless, our route comes down to Loch a'Chairn Bhain (Cairnbawn) and Kylesku.

From here, the A894 goes to the eastern end of *Loch Assynt* where the route joins the A807 to *Ledmore*, *Oykel* and *Lairg*. Alternatively, a shorter route can be followed at Laxford Bridge by keeping to the A838 which passes Loch More and then returns to Lairg along the north side of Loch Shin.

Gazetteer

ACHILTIBUIE
A solitary little community west of Coigach and facing the Summer Isles. Tanera More, the largest island, protects the bay. Good views of the Coigach mountains on and across the bay to An Teallach on Loch Broom.

DURNESS
Crofting village in remote situation above Sango Bay, which has a superb beach. Though small, Durness has two hotels to accommodate the visitors who want to enjoy this remote northern coast, and a Craft Centre.

Visit:
Balnakiel, a few scattered houses by the beach beyond the Craft Village. The ruined 17th-century chapel, Durness Old Church, belonged to the Lords Reay;
Balnakiel Craft Village, 1 mile W of Durness, has a dozen different craft businesses. Open daily Apr-Sept;
Smoo Cave, three caverns, second one has a waterfall, the third is not accessible. Open daily most of the year.

INCHNADAMPH
A hotel (with one of the few petrol pumps in the region), a few isolated houses and Assynt Church make up Inchnadamph at the eastern end of Loch Assynt.
Visit:
The Allt nan Uamh Caves, 2½ miles SE of Inchnadamph in a large nature reserve, were inhabited by primitive man and today are explored by speleologists.

LAIRG
Small town at the south-east end of Loch Shin, at meeting place of roads from north, east and west: wild Highlands to the north, and pretty Shin valley to Bonar Bridge. Good hotel and other accommodation.
Visit:
Carbisdale Castle, an impressive Edwardian pile by the railway, near the junction of the River Shin and the River Oykel. Carbisdale is near the site of Montrose's defeat by Cromwell's army before he became a prisoner at Ardvreck Castle. View from the outside only;
Falls of Shin, to the south of Lairg, rush over rocks in deep wooded gorge. Salmon leap.

LOCHINVER
Village and fishing port in Coigach where the River Inver flows into the sea at a sheltered harbour. Centre for walking and climbing among the mountains of Coigach.

Visit:
Inverpolly National Nature Reserve where deer, wildcats and eagles are among the wild life. Good views of Stac Polly, Cul Mor and Cul Beag. Information Centre open Mon-Fri, May-Sept.

SCOURIE
Attractive little crofting village in a green valley surrounded by rocky, treeless country. Handa Island can be reached from Scourie.

SUMMER ISLES
Group of islands off Achiltibuie from where motorboats make trips to the island during the summer months. The innermost and largest island is Tanera Mor which, like the other islands, is now uninhabited and has a plentiful bird life. Other islands are Tanera Beag and Horse Island. The latter has wild goats and is reputed to contain buried pirate's treasure.

ULLAPOOL
The largest resort in the north-west has several hotels and good facilities for sailing and fishing on Loch Broom. A good centre for touring and walking. Steamer services to the Hebrides leave from Ullapool pier.

Visit:
The Corrieshalloch Gorge, 200 ft deep, is along the A824 and contains the Falls of Measach which are specially impressive in spring after rain;
Cross the loch to Aultnaharrie where there is a pleasant little hotel and good views of Ullapool and the Coigach Mountains.